Free Will

OTHER BOOKS BY HAROLD RHENISCH

Poetry

Winter, Sono Nis Press, 1982

Eleusis, Sono Nis Press, 1986

A Delicate Fire, Sono Nis Press, 1989

Dancing With My Daughter, Sono Nis Press, 1993

In the Presence of Ghosts, Reference West, 1993

Iodine, Wolsak & Wynn, 1994

Taking the Breath Away, Ronsdale Press, 1998

The Blue Mouth of Morning, Oolichan Books, 1998

Kazoo: The Psalm at the End of the Song, Reference West, 1998

Fusion, Exile Editions, 1999

On the Couch of Dr. Daydream: Shakespeare by Rhenisch,
Greenboathouse, 2001

Bioregional Essays

Out of the Interior: the Lost Country, Cacanadadada Press, 1993

Tom Thomson's Shack. New Star Books, 2000

Fiction

Carnival, Porcupine's Quill, 2000

Translations

Peyote, or My Friend the Indian, by Stefan Schütz,
Ronsdale Press, 2001

Free Will

- poems on stage -

Harold Rhenisch

RONSDALE PRESS

FREE WILL
Copyright © 2004 Harold Rhenisch

RONSDALE PRESS
3350 West 21st Avenue
Vancouver, B.C., Canada
V6S 1G7

Edited by Ronald B. Hatch
Typesetting: Julie Cochrane, in New Baskerville 11 pt on 13.5
Cover Design: Sandie Drzewiecki
Cover Art: John Hagan, "Shakespeare Looking at Shakespeare"
Author Photo: Leandra Rhenisch

Ronsdale Press wishes to thank the Canada Council for the Arts, the Government of Canada through the Book Publishing Industry Development Program (BPIDP), and the Province of British Columbia through the British Columbia Arts Council for their support of its publishing program.

National Library of Canada Cataloguing in Publication

Rhenisch, Harold, 1958–
    Free will / Harold Rhenisch.

    Poems.
    ISBN 1-55380-013-3

    I. Title.

PS8585.H54F74 2004   C811'.54   C2003-907357-2

Printed in Canada by Hignell Book Printing

CONTENTS

for Stefan Schütz

PUN INTENDED

—

"The clown is the center of the ceremony"
– Stefan Schütz, *Peyote*

This book began in 1975, when I drove off the farm to Victoria
in a 1957 Ford Sedan with four colours of paint and a bullet
hole in the back window. Who knows where the bullet hole had
come from. I bought that old beater off my brother for $150.
He used the money to buy himself a Honda 450, with a crash
bar and lots of chrome. He was into *Easy Rider*. I was off to play
Puck in A *Midsummer Night's Dream,* on the strength of a passion
for the absurdist theatre of Ionesco. I thought it best not to ask
about the bullet. Slipping the blue toque off my long golden
hair and clearing my head of Leonard Cohen's "Songs of Love
and Hate," which were rolling around in there like a piece of
gravel in a hubcap, I thumped around a minimalist set for six
weeks, speaking spells, making magic, and acting that I was act-
ing. Fifteen years later, I woke up with a start in the middle of
the night, sweating, repeating lines from the play, but this time
voicing them as they cried to be voiced — singing, laughing

them out, teasing, calling, taunting. The dreams, if they were dreams, continued for years. I was no longer acting.

The result is this book. Shakespeare rattles around in it, as he does in my head, with his fools and lovers, his cross-dressers, his heroes who aren't heroes, his tragedies that aren't tragedies, his comedies that often have more in common with Monty Python and *La Cage aux Folles* than with high art. Ionesco is never far behind. The whole avalanche of poetry that has come down off the mountain of Purgatory with surrealists skiing madly before it, absurdist playwrights digging up somnambulist lyricists, and visual poets and sound poets tramping in with their dogs and their barrels of brandy, end up tumbling into the après-ski chalet of this book, where Puck tends bar. Here, though, their stunt acts and special effects, a world of hallucinatory dreams and silent-movie utopias, are brought back to the world of reason, and bed it.

Puck is a fairy, a trickster, the one who stands outside of all stories and causes them to take place, capriciously. He is also a trick himself, a piece of sleight-of-hand. Shakespeare-Houdini, that master of mirrors and disguise, set up his sonnets as Chinese boxes. The only escape from them is the point at which physical and spiritual love cross. In the same spirit of pulling rabbits — or himself — out of hats, Shakespeare set up his plays as mazes of mirrors, out of which there is only one avenue of escape: theatre — a thing as light as air. Rapacious, driven, compulsive, unpredictable, impulsive, vital, frightening, transient, sexually ambiguous, and dangerous, Puck is the creative imagination itself. The card huckster that is Puck has his own mirrors, too: Lear, who mocks himself; the sinister but smiling Iago; the indecisive Hamlet, who plays his own fools. They differ from Puck only because the space created for them forces their energy into different straight jackets, as our different bodies do to our own souls. United by an urge to live, and to live freely, these characters fight their fate — Will Shakespeare, who penned them in. By pulling the rug of tragedy out from under their feet, he is forcing them, the actors who play them, and any of the others of us who let them pound the boards in our minds, to think for ourselves, and to free him, Will, from death. The plays are great, complex, incantatory and alchemical engines. God help us all.

Any combination of reason and unreason is absurd, of course. The city of this book is populated by clowns and fools. Punch, Coyote, Charlie Chaplin, Robin Goodfellow, Black Adder, Marcel Marceau, and the shriners on their scooters in small town parades, all take their turns behind the camera, directing a scene from the show. The tragedy is common to them all — Shakespeare and his audience trapped within the house of mirrors of their minds, finding escape by putting on masks of themselves. In each scene, the mind shows up in a different mirror, each poem a different glint of light cast off a forest leaf or a stream in moonlight. In irreverent reverence, every poem collected here circles around, fills, and ultimately retreats from silence, a finger on its lips. Randomness, and the ability of the mind to outrun its snapping jaws, to dance around it, daring it to do its worst, is all. Reason, in this universe, is not a prison.

This vision of Puck has roots in the old definition of infinity: if you were to lock 10,000 monkeys in a room with 10,000 typewriters, they would eventually write *Hamlet*. In this book, they do — and a lot of other plays besides: comedies, tragedies, romances, histories, gallows humour, the works. These lab chimps finally get their own say, free of surgical implants and double-blind controls. In their plays, though, as in Shakespeare's own, the tragedies are not about tragic heroes. Instead, they detail the repercussions of tragedy upon people, how it constrains them, and how, by joy, delight and by playing roles they can be released from the cage of living alone in a vast, unknowable universe, where scientists wear identification badges and white coats and bring medications on steel trays. *Hamlet* is not Hamlet's play, for instance, but Ophelia's. Her play appears here, stripped of Shakespeare's distorting lens that gave us Hamlet's story instead. Iago's play is here as well. So is Puck's. And Desdemona's. Here, too, are actors identifying with their parts until the two are indistinguishable. The stage becomes the audience, the audience the actors on the stage. A new sequence is added to Shakespeare's sonnets, bringing them into the world of prime time sitcoms and cop shows. The major genres — and some minor ones — of western literature are put on stage, to do their vaudeville act, and Puck makes his magic, or reaches out his hook. In this universe, the subconscious mind will not be contained and takes equal stage with its conscious twin. I call that art. Shakespeare appears, dressed in the monstrous garb of free will. It is the choice he can offer. The magic is real. In offering my version of Shakespeare's choice, I have followed Puck's lead.

Welcome to the show!

ROMANCE

—

Seems, Madam? I know not seems.
— Hamlet

Telling the Truth

[handwritten annotations: "A", "Theyre asking the wrong question", "linked to p94 p16, p26, revised of this one"]

When someone asks you for the truth,
for God's sake, lie. Give them what they want.

And if they ask again, lie a second time,
a third, a fourth, until you're hoarse;

sign every paper they slide across to you,
their finger on the line, where they ask you

for your house, your car, your stocks;
pay the interest on your debt, accept the truth,

stand before the camera and tell them how it was,
how it's all true — you blew up that bridge,

stole those plans, took your boss's wife
to Palm Beach — for you have been to Hell

and back these last few weeks, and deserve
no less than an end to lies, fine print,

and sound bites, not to mention sleep,
what with all you've had to swallow

just to stand here in my place and defend
those actions you know nothing of,

denied a chance to say what you do know,
while I stand in for you, with my briefcase

and my files, whispering in your ear, that what
you say in this court matters not,

that you know yourself at last (I squeeze
your arm), that truth is a lie.

The Hall of Mirrors

Things aren't what they seem.
Right now you look eight feet tall,

while I, beside you, am a dwarf.
I come up to your knees and grin.

A minute ago I was fat and heavy
and you were my twin,

and further down the hall
here in the dark we will both

be impossibly thin, like two trees
that have put on rags or two scarecrows in a garden,

their blind eyes mad with birds,
that whirl and peck the crop

before we can take it in.
We came here for some fun,

so let's have it. Oh look,
here around the corner our bones are bent,

our heads don't sit where we're used
to seeing them, but off to the side,

and our spines, that should hold us up straight
as our mothers always told us, tucking us in,

are bent like lightning forking down to a lone
elm in a field and splitting it.

We should both fall down,
but don't. We move on,

straighten out, shrink, twist, and laugh
at what we see, not because we're having fun

but because I have forgotten what I am:
man, or tree or twisted thing that jumps

up in the dark. When I look at you,
you're no help, as I'd hoped you'd be —

the mirrors reflect you as well.
We came in here knowing who we were,

and still know it. It's who we are that's troubling.
Things are what they seem.

The Uncollected Sonnets of Mr. W.S., Translated from the English

SONNET 155: THE HEIST

I've got to hand it to you, the way you pulled it off:
despite all the guards, the cameras, the infrared,

you stole my heart, that sparkled like cut glass.
Now security has brought in tracking dogs,

dusted for fingerprints, and put word out
on the street to find the thief. Like the rest, I say

I don't know who did this deed — except I lie.
The gallery is empty, the lights turned up;

men with coveralls search with microscopes;
I should lock myself in Nice and weep,

but I just can't. Right now my heart is racing
through Beirut. We came in at night — a fishing boat.

The salt was sharp. The dark swells
were a shock. I shuddered in delight. Ah,

there's the shop, a door in back, a gentle knock,
three times like a bird cracking a nut, and we're

inside. I can barely stand it, the way we walk — I say *we*,
but I am carried, I know, and the man in black

is walking, with sure footsteps on the carpet —
towards soft words, cups of tea, bright light. Ah,

I am laid out on a velvet pillow, and you
pick me up at last and hold me up,

beloved. Your heart is stolen too,
you thief, don't tell me it isn't.

SONNET 156: THE GATE

I hope you got it all on film, the way we moved
in that half-light as sirens blared

out on the street and neon flashed
on grey walls from the strip club

down below. You stood five minutes by the window,
the curtains pulled to see the fight

the cops put up, the pools of blood, the crack
dealers come back and pick right up

where they'd left off. You turned,
as naked as, well, if not Eve, at least

as Gabriel, the judge, the sword, the life,
the gate that we must guard

or pass, and laughed. The whole time
I was bound and could only watch,

gagged, and drugged by the sight of you
and by my lust. You had me then, pulled

the bindings off, dressed me up, then let
me go at you, and I did, with relish, the red light

flashing as we loved that night, the morning streets
washed clean of blood, the dealers gone

to sleep it off, not like us. We were up.
We looked for eggs to swallow whole

before going down to rule the lives
that we take off.

SONNET 157: IN THE LINEUP

I am in the lineup with other thieves
and dealers from the street,

in the glare of light. You stand
behind the mirror with a Styrofoam cup

of coffee and the pigs, who grunt at us
through the mic, *Turn to the left*

(It's like a line dance in a country hall.
I throw back my head and sashay up.)

and *Have the short one step forward*
and blow a kiss. I'm caught! I sweat

and step out of the line, knowing you undress me
right there, in front of the cops, the crooks,

the guards. They probably have the whole thing
spooled on tape. When you leave, they'll give

you a copy of the cassette, which you
can play at home whenever you want

to watch me twist, but what I want
to know is when you caught that kiss

on your cruel cheek, did you want to rush down
swept by laughter or did you think instead,

Tie him up!, because I can't stand here
much longer without a charge in court,

and if I'm going to plead guilty I need to know what
sentence you will give, or do I get house arrest?

SONNET 158: BROADSIDE

I didn't see it coming, that notice in the press:
you're no longer responsible for my debts:

your attorney's phone, your maiden name,
mine in bold type. Why not post it on every stall

so women could read it while they flush?
Maiden! Now that's a joke — or maybe miracles

are happening now and we can all go back
to the years of stuttering hesitation

before we knew the apple rots
if not picked, and we all know that.

You've been picked, and eaten,
and I spit you out. I came home from work

to find the house empty, the floors echoing,
the curtains limp, the bank account drained

and my VISA blocked, for what?
That you didn't love me, that I was a mistake?

Darling — if I can talk to what you once were —
you're the one who's mistaken here;

love's not like that, the gentle evenings
where our dreams are one,

the dusty pages of a book, slowly
turned; it's this: our hate.

SONNET 159: UP AGAINST THE WALL

Let's have no secrets.
I will be the one who talks;

you can be the one with ropes and lights.
I'll tell you everything you ask,

sign documents you shove across,
and act so well that you will spit

in my face, and only when the table's turned
and I strip off the ropes, pull on the black

hood and lead you out before the wall
as grey pigeons rise up in the dawn

as if the buildings were taking flight,
will I forgive, have my men

lay their rifles down and carry you in,
where I will wash your welts and you

wash mine with tears and kisses,
and, fingers trembling, will escape this hell

where we're apart and can only meet like this,
at first not knowing that it's us,

then the shock that what we know
and what we signed we have never done,

but would a hundred times
to tell the honest truth.

Without a Clue

I started without a clue of who killed the guest
in the highland castle by the loch,

with the salmon rising under the ice of the burn
that sang all summer over rills,

the foxes running through the snow
and heather burning on the fire.

It is a land of ghosts, of men betrayed,
a people sold to foreign power,

water steeped in peat and set aside
in burnt oak for all the years

of a woman's beauty,
the lonely walks across the moor,

the bracing wind, and women,
who don't pray to gods or God, and men

who say they do, but pray
to themselves instead,

expecting an answer when they kneel
before an altar of devotion,

while women wait — not theirs in the least —
between ironed sheets,

too cold to sleep. My experience so far
in this distant place as near as kin

is none will come.
The place drives men apart.

The women talk of lives past
and lives to come as if they're past

and only speech is left before a fire.
Men drink the smoke.

The obsequious butler, the retired India man
who knows enough of slaughter,

the starlet from the south, who pretends
to know the nothing the wisest know

is the nothing that will slay them in the end,
and all the other guests, the poet,

who rhymes the heather with the weather,
(he drinks too much champagne

and cries for attention),
the medium (the accent's fake),

the prime minister (retired),
the mayor from the village,

who talks too loud, the prince
(a case study for any kid who's reading Freud),

all know that one of them is marked for death,
that their presence is a crime they will commit

and so must answer to, no matter how they struggle
to turn it to laughter as candles dance

above a table set with silver
and crystal goblets and claret.

The pheasant steams, the windows set with lead,
such tiny panes, each one leaking wind.

The fox is wild. The night is his.
All know it, and laugh to forget.

The stars that rise blue above the snow
and fall through fog are the cold men know

in those dark halls, but not the cold
that drives the fox, and not the cold of God.

That is the cold we come to in the end.
We're not there yet, but we are close.

It is the women, dressed in red,
who throw the heather on and smell it burn

even in their sleep, if they can sleep
with no warmth but their own

between the sheets and dream
the dream that is all that is.

The Escape

When I started I knew nothing about this,
its boards, its lice, the bright
anguish of its nights, the long hours
lying in the hut hearing bones sleep,
men cough out their lives, while light
swept over walls in shadows,
and delighted words showed me the devices
they would use to get the truth,
for it's truth they want and truth
the one thing I cannot give. Even this
is a lie, to throw them off, a hacksaw
in a cake, meat for the dogs
they keep, a message to the others
who have tunnelled here for months, *Tonight*.

Eat this note. The words are smart.
If they catch us they have an injection
for the heart. Do what they say. When questioned,
tell the truth, that you know nothing about this,
that you aren't crazy; there are no others;
you spoke to no one. There is no escape
from the truth. Tell them that.

COMEDY

—

I am only mad North-Northwest.
   – Hamlet

The Great White Hope: the End of an Era

Magic Lantern Show

(Punch + Judy)

Punch is fighting through the jungle
with a bowler hat and a cane.
In a steady stream behind him,
porters are carrying champagne,
deck chairs, a folding
canvas tent, a gramophone.
They are pasted to a loop;
they come back again and again
in the same order — some tall, some stooped —
while Punch draws lines on a map
that a minute ago was a page in a book
of poems by Francis Thompson
about the magical East
of incense and jewels
and Asia resplendent in Time.

He does not see the crocodile,
the gorilla, the baboon;
he steps on the croc's head,
passes his elephant gun
to the gorilla for a sec,
while he adjusts his hat,
asks the baboon for a tall stiff drink
to take the heat from the afternoon.
Pretty soon they're all behind him,
tiptoeing at the back of his train.
While he says, *I have discovered this country,*
and twirls his cane,
a band of howler monkeys does the Charleston,
and that's that —

until the audience comes,
with all their words in lower case
and their mornings behind them.

They cheer most for the crocodile.
You old suitcase! they cry
as he snaps at Punch's trousers,
until the gorilla snatches the hat,
dances before Punch,
holding it at the tip of his fingers
and finally throwing it into the crowd.
What we believe, is real.

The baboon is the philosopher.
He sits against the side of the stage and eats
a banana from a heavy bunch
that gets lowered from the heavens.
When he's finished he places the peel
on Punch's head: a hat.
Like that, they walk off,

leaving the crowd to their afternoons,
as the porters go round and round
with their Caruso and their silver plate,
the only sun they know shining on them
from the centre of their ring: 60 watts.

What We Believe, is Real

Puppet Theater

Look right now! What did I tell you?
There is a devil dressed in red!
He looks six inches tall,
his tail slithering behind him
like a fuse on a bomb. Oh no! He has a pretty
young woman with hair as yellow
as plastic flowers under his arm now
and he is dragging her off!

She is putting up a pretty good fight.
There are children sitting in the grass
in front of her, screaming, *Stop it! Put her down!*
Eeeeee!, but doing nothing about it,
although it would seem easy enough
to run behind the sky to snatch the strings
and do away with the devil altogether,
so the woman could have a quiet moment
in which to sing all the songs she's ever wanted —
the new moon with the old moon in her arms,
the roses of springtime.

The children scream so much they're laughing,
while the devil can't get enough.
He drags the woman back a second time;
he tries to kiss her. Just in time, a clown comes,
with a tear painted on his cheek and royal blue lips.
He chases the devil away, with a plastic flower on his lapel
that squirts water. The children on the grass are squealing.
Ha ha! Get him! Give him a great big kiss! He does!

The clown has the devil in his arms,
the tail looped over his shoulder.
They dance a tango cheek to cheek,
while the woman pouts
and sighs too loudly. It goes on like this for hours —
the hero comes on, the hero goes off,
the woman falls into the earth and rises again,
as the sky, the earth. Children, we believe.

10,000 Monkeys Locked in a Room

When the chimps were brought together
into a hall in Soho,
grinning and somersaulting,
leapfrogging, jumping jacks,
and rudely imitating
simple sexual acts,

each given a pine table,
a typewriter, a chair
on casters and a stack
of blank paper,
they pounded the keys —
with the tips of their fingers,
elbows, knees,
or each of their toes individually.

Some typed nothing,
picked nits, groomed, nursed
their young or stared blankly
out of their captivity;
others attacked the Olivettis,
the Coronas, the Underwoods —
jumping on the keys, filling whole pages
with semi-colons and ampersands.

Technicians in white lab coats
and soft-soled shoes
passed among them,
tearing A4 paper from rollers,
in the ding of the returns,
the hollering and jubilation.

In the midst of pages,
sections, volumes, shelves,
libraries, catacombs of nonsense,
and those other pages
on which the monkeys had defecated,
urinated, spat, blew snot,
reams they had chewed into spitballs,
each carefully unfolded and laid in the albums —
in this orgy of etiquette —

the chimpanzees of Soho
had written *Hamlet:* to be
or not to be, the skull
lifted from the grave, sick
jokes with undertakers,
the late night drinking,
the borders leaking like a sieve.

The press came in squadrons.
Little sausages were served
on stainless steel platters.
The chimps all wore lace collars
like the ones Shakespeare starched
when he went to visit the Queen
who turned her lovers into pirates
and had them served in her tower.

Some scenes were apocryphal:
Ophelia wasn't buried; Hamlet was.
He had been stabbed. Polonius did it,
the old jackboot. And Rosencrantz
and Guildenstern thought better of driving north
in their Volvo into Denmark
during the second winter of the Occupation.

The only thing the chimps
got consistently right was the drinking.
From the first word, even the ghost was drunk,
teetering on the parapet. He could hardly
hold himself together, leaning back
to take a leak, pissing himself away.

The city was in an uproar. For weeks
people brought bananas and pawpaws,
hacks slipped papers into the monkey cages,
collected them later, rushed them in taxis
to black-oiled presses before a russet dawn
licked its paws; they were shipped across the city
and into the farthest sheep farms;
everyone bought the first editions;
the headlines were outlandish:
Motorcycle Takes to the Skies at Aerodrome,
Parliament Discusses Spinach.
Business ground to a halt. The boys and girls
in white jackets ran a gauntlet of paparazzi.
Their tongues tasted like flash bulbs.
Their photos appeared in the most scurrilous rags,
with monkey heads crudely pasted on;
you could see the scissor marks;
they weren't to scale. The King and Queen,
the ones who had no pirates and no lovers,
looked out on a city on flame.

When the janitor discovered waste paper crumpled
into balls, tossed, rebounded — the lousy
free throws of one lab chimp who had crawled
into a closet with the Smith Corona, the boys
and girls were shocked. It was a detailed plan
for the invasion of England — everyone
who was anyone was on a list to be shot;
the new king was Fortinbras. On the next sheet,
Fortinbras had fallen from favour: Ophelia
was Queen in his place; she dissolved the monarchy,
opened a sex shop on Leicester Square.
On the next page, she was dropped — a republic
was founded, a consortium of bankers,
a fragile language without a king.

"Which is better?" the chimp had begun,
"to be a slave or to be a free man enslaved,
to be a man in his city or a chimp,
even if his jungle is the dictionary —
that leg hold trap, that artemesia,
that cognitive turnip, that that?"

transference of pur
- monkeys fur
we're mushy

The Lost and Found Play

One week the librarian unlocked the halls
to discover, to the depths of his blue-lit lungs,

swirling with cigar smoke,
in the deeps where Churchill had been born,

swaddled in light, mewling,
blind and hairless, every book

had been written in code. To decipher
this code he has devoted his life

from this point forward. With blackboards and dictionaries,
flow charts, laser pointers, the librarian

brought a hidden play to light, reading
between the lines of the monkeys' *Hamlet:* a wounded play,

a toothpick snapped between the teeth — Kate
and Petruccio wrestling on the stage,

sweat pouring down. The referee
is a chimpanzee in black and white,

with a whistle and a shaving cream grin. When
Kate is up against the ropes, the crowd howls.

When Petruccio is on the mat,
they stand and clap. All the while,

money passes hands. The odds are fixed
at ten to one. The smart money says Kate will win.

It is always that way now. In their staging
of *The Tempest* last week,

the chimps painted the sorcerer green, gave him a cloak
woven of pages torn from books

bound in vellum,
ate the vellum.

They had a central committee
that decided all matters of taste:

cauliflower (blah), turnips (blah),
kohlrabi (yuck, yuck, yuck);

but the taste of Miranda's lips
in her cloak of morning,

the shift of her hip
the lilt of her head (tiralee!) —

for that they swept the table clean
and got down to work

with both fingers and toes:
160 words per minute (cha cha cha!),

on machines that had just gone through
the fourth rewrite of *Lear* —

some with bent keys, the big Olivetti
without the letter N,

or periods. The committee decided everything:
who would recount the story

of the green chimpanzee
thrown into a cage, smelling of paint,

how the other cellmates
tore him to shreds,

hammered on the bars with his limbs,
spattering the jailors in their white coats;

how to frame the injustice;
what form the retribution would take:

Ariel was locked in a tree trunk
and made to eat the key;

the sorcerer was afraid to show himself;
Ferdinand was turned into a bull,

given a slap on the rump,
and led out to pasture.

There was no talk about lovers:
Caliban became the new duke;

Miranda the duchess —
everyday she forgot one word more

than she had forgotten the day before,
a forgetfulness so complete

each word forgotten was the first.
There were five-year plans,

industrial quotas; coffee was passed,
spilled, wiped off with the forearm,

licked up; committee members
hung from the lights. By the time

they caught the sorcerer, pressed
him between the pages of the book

like a forget-me-not,
he had packed a cardboard suitcase

and was headed out of town.
The chimps laughed, they smiled,

they nodded, they obliged; one
swung down and wrote in a train for him,

puffing out of King's Cross
with a cargo of soldiers in muddy brown

cheering on their way to Flanders,
throwing caps into the air,

each with a stalk of broccoli in his lapel:
hurrah! three cheers for bangers and mash!

for Piccadilly and late night toddies
when the children are in bed like carrots

and me and the missus
play doctor and nurse!

As soon as the sorcerer boarded,
pushing his suitcase ahead of himself

(compartment doors slamming, hard stares;
in one compartment a crew of chimpanzees

making faces in the glass;
the sorcerer fighting his way down the crowded corridor) —

the chimp tore the train from the machine
and crumpled it up.

The partisans at the committee table nodded,
drew up the next schedule,

reviewed last fall's grain production,
wrote themselves a storm.

The world heaved in the troughs,
its mast splintering. The monkeys lay in the hold,

arm in arm, staring up at the deck
in the darkness, in anticipation

of how a play could write itself
when a play could write itself on its own.

The Missing Man of the Congo

My generation first read *Othello* in the tabloids,
where Desdemona was a missionary's daughter
and Othello was a mercenary protecting
the diamond trade a thousand miles upriver.
The lovers hadn't read Kingsolver.
Not once did they see the chimpanzees,
hiding in blinds of bamboo and malaria,
observing their caresses, making notes,
writing out with professional detachment
the slow rise of their love
and its quick fall.

We did. The chimps were supplying rainbow condoms
with pleasure ribs. They sprinkled "An Evening in Paris"
on Desdemona's ear, polished Othello's buttons
(solid brass), made such a racket in the bush
he had to protect her: the rest is history —

but whose? We didn't care. We plunked
down our cash, so we could read the script
firsthand, printed in facsimile — a concoction
of scribbles, drawings of birds, leaf outlines,
handprints, drops of blood, spit
and squished bugs. We clamoured for more.
We had been longing for this for decades,
ever since the sacred monkeys of the monastery at Hue
and the monks who became smoke in lacquered bowls.

Soon we could all speak like that,
in clicks and hand signals, guttural squeaks,
tracings of insect wings across sand. The chimps
from the language institutes were guests
on late night talk shows and entertained their hosts
with witty tricks and long bouts of melancholy,
told insider jokes from the Washington martini circuit,
and when Letterman began to look uneasy
grinned broadly to set him at ease,
with breath that smelled of orchids.

Pretty soon we were all watching each other.
Binoculars were sold out at the Army Surplus —
night vision scopes, kids' plastic periscopes.
Shakespeare was completely out of the picture,
Conrad had gone to sleep in his malaria,
Kingsolver was put to bed in a corn field in Iowa,
with the remaindered copies of her Congo
spread round her like rose petals, and when everyone
was pretty much comfortable with their new roles
with each other and had the right distance from the script,
it was a shame that no one had thought to look for Iago,
with his ivories and his hooked nose and his gin,
because his part had been completely written out,
and he was writing it back in.

Iago's Version

Backstage, the birds were everywhere — nuthatches
                                    and lyre birds,
eagles and grosbeaks. Starlings fluttered in Romeo's face,
twittering like children in the Gaza Strip.
Romeo couldn't slay Tybalt — he couldn't see him.
Nightingales hung onto the rose arbour and trilled
                                    like violins.
When Juliet cried, *A rose by any other name*
would smell as sweet, Romeo heard the birds
and saw the moon with its hollow corpse's face, puckering.

Othello rolled over — on his pillow there was a shrike
that had flown from the Euphrates with a ball of mud.
You couldn't hold down a conversation.
It was fine for an evening,
but it went on for years.

After a decade, none of us thought anymore.
Actors swung around lamp posts.
They sang "Singing in the Rain"
in a language made of grunts and squeaks.
They picked lice. They made love in public.
They carried their children on their backs.
They slept on their roofs under the stars
while the monkeys moved among them
with bullwhips and serums,
writing everything down meticulously,
asdrilk&8()(* with ashtray, Bonsai with %%^/1jd,
but no-one could read it, except God,
and for him it was the book of the world.
He lived within it. He wanted a door,

yet wherever he looked out through long rooms,
the ceiling fans framed against
the black grates of the balconies,
there was an ostrich or a heron or a kite.

There were so many parrots, he couldn't see past them:
he had a thousand doors; there was no way out
that was not blocked by peahens and bitterns
which had become a sentence
in a syntax that would not end.

For every improvised scene the librarians cut
from the chimpanzees' manuscripts —
the scene of Rosalind reading *Chatelaine*
while having her nails done, the scene of Shylock
eating kosher dills in a Montreal deli —
our world backstage became more empty,
more like a wind blowing from the farthest stars
across the keys of Bach's harpsichord,
chilling his fingers; less like a world at all.

The scene of Oberon fitting his rainbow codpiece, cut,
the scene of Falstaff planting tobacco in Virginia, cut —
until there was just one last scrap of a scene
in the bottom of the in-tray. The librarians lifted it out,
turned it over, read it backwards, forwards,
the light of trees washing over their faces,
branches swaying in wind five minutes after rain,
read it until there was nothing left of it,
until the letters were all invisible,
having passed from this world into the mind.

What had been a play lay before them in ruins.
They poked at it with a pen —
the image of monkeys laughing on one scrap of paper.
When they looked at it directly, there was nothing.
They had to catch it out of the corner of an eye.

So is it possible to see the world outside of reason,
the light playing on the edge of a room,
rain passing in chainlink sheets
across the face of a spring mountain,
the scent of pine needles, and actors looking up
to see clouds, forming in living air,
dissipate in the wind,
and reading themselves there.

The Northwest Passage

the hand of Franklin
reaching for the Beaufort Sea.
           – Stan Rogers

The Saskatchewan River
is a glacier flowing to the sea
at the speed of time —

a speed so slow
that for us it is solid matter
and we are the ones who move;

but it is incandescent.

What is happening in this play
is not at the speed of time.

What is happening in this play
is unfolding in a white-out.

In the first scene a circus
is stranded on a Winnipeg siding.
Snow flashes past: TV static.
Tigers pace on ice. Monkeys
huddle in a corner, whimpering.
Snow drifts over frozen lettuce.
The keepers are drunk. They stagger,
hunched against driving snow.
In this play snow falls horizontally.
The manuscript is a white stack of paper,
blowing in our faces.

The players' parts are what the characters do not say
in the version that hit the wooden stage
with golden costumes and beggars.
"Regan, pass me the salt." *We can't afford salt.*
What's the matter with my cooking?
Why do you want salt? You haven't even tasted it.
"Goneril, I need fresh towels in my ensuite.
Get your own fucking towels. This isn't a hotel.
And you can just forget about hot water.
"Fool, when I beat you
I feel I am striking myself."
Lord, when I joke with you,
I am joking with myself.

Snow has blown all the way
from Winnipeg to Red Deer.
It has drifted against fences.
On the highways, traffic has snowed in.
The audience is huddled in icy hulls,
each with an emergency candle and a blanket.
In this play every actor is alone on a vast earth.

I Miss the Cold War, Darling

But look, the morn in russet mantle clad
Walks o'er the dew of yon high eastward hill.
– Horatio

I miss the day I walked through Copenhagen
in the yellow light, that hung before me
within the air, chatting with Hamlet
in the stage of my mind, the words like rapiers,
as Chernobyl fell over my shoulders
and I breathed the graphite furnaces
deep into my lungs
and set him to coughing.
Then I was standing at the station.
There were no trains rolling out
or rolling in, but the food was heaped
three feet high on the tables
and Polonius was at the door
in a starched white shirt
to take my fifty crowns. Later that night,
I walked back to the hotel
through coal-stained streets,
with shadows of red neon,

to the attic I shared with
a violinist and a soprano and a baby
sleeping on the floor, or rather not sleeping,
nor was I, nobody was sleeping — Ophelia was dancing
naked in the window
of a bar on the corner, red
light, darkness, red light
darkness, a drum

holding a beat under electric music.
All that time the children of Chernobyl
were burning in my lungs.
The Cold War gave us meaning
and purpose. It said
what was clear and we were its shadow.

In the new world, I find old pictures of Kristallnacht,
synagogues in the Murtal,
small towns nestled against black mountains,
going up in fountains of flame;
all around children and firemen watch,
like a bloody wiener roast up my Ashnola River,
with corn on the cob and cold trout in an eddy,
the whole town up there away from the heat,
peach trees boughed to the grass,
as the light hung green
between the hills in the evenings,
and today a coyote with three legs
loped across the highway into the aspens,
twisted, rubbed bare by cattle.

Men with faces of charcoal and stumps for arms,
the stars pour through our hands like water
splashed on the face with a shout:
it wasn't the Russians who led the war against us;
there wasn't even a war, only the cold
rimming the edge of a finger,
a line of barbed wire stretching into distance,
a stream in the high country:
storm that blanked out the world
as the dogs barked and the russet hills
answered with the hills.

Hamlet: The Player and the Part

We have come now to the edge of time.
I dress in black and take the stage, knife in hand,
to kill the king, who prays to God
with words he's known for weeks,
and practised, to make them sound convincing.

For my part, we talked it over and blocked
it out: I'd come in here, exit here, and in between
I would be afraid to become the king
I killed and so would sheathe my knife
and stage a play, so the court would see
themselves as fools, for wisdom does not dress
in authority, but comes with bells
tied to its feet, and mocks and jibes.

Do you believe that anymore? The clown
may be the ceremony, but a stage
is a mirror, that shows not the world,
but what is. We know the world is not,
the king's a lie, and I refuse, as others have
(it's in the script), to play this part,
because the time is up, the kingdom's rotten
and the young are married to your mind.

Dead girl, dead father, dead king (two),
dead queen, dead prince, dead friend, all dead,
dead, dead, dead, dead. I should have ended
it when I could! Now, hold your hands
and bow and let the people clap
at what they think they've seen,
what we've played and what's played
us out and having played returns
to silence and broods.

TRAGEDY

—

Whither wilt thou lead me? Speak;
I'll go no further.
— Hamlet

Playing Macbeth in the City of Fools

It is the opening night
of the Scottish play.
The river has surged
over its banks.
Carp swim through the salons
in the old quarter.
The public library is clotted with eels,
turning and writhing,
but up on the hill
Macbeth is Thane,
accepting the chains
and ancient kinship.

All through the city
fools rush through rising water
to the doors of the theatre,
dripping wet, sneezing.
Some strip off their clothes
and sit in glory;
they sprawl in red velvet
and laugh in gloom.
Some recite poems.
Some say the moon
is flowing with floodwater;
the trout are laying eggs
among stars and planets,
thrusting up cold gravel
with aluminum tails.

Shhh! the jester calls,
shaking his bells,
as Lady Macbeth
washes thin hands.
This is the best part!

Still the waters rise,
still more fools walk out of drowning streets,
all the business of their lives floating around them —
pictures of vacations in Greece, Aunt Ida
at a meeting of the Empire Club in London,
with the silver service and the Waterford crystal,
sodden books, scores of symphonies, umbrellas.

They push in, laughing and jabbering,
shaking themselves dry. The actors
are completely unheard among the babble —
they shout until they're hoarse.
In the end, they go through a dumb show
until the rising storm breaks and the blowing
forests march out of the dawn
the cool branches rising and settling down —
flags above a battlefield, shredded voices.

The faces in the audience stare up at Macbeth,
raging. He sees them for the first time.
They watch him without hope,
their lips twisted, their eyes sly,
their hair matted with flotsam.

They are shouting words he cannot hear,
laughing in derision,
the closest tugging at his clothes,
splashing as they move,
pushing with strong thighs.

Soon the bright-eyed and the lame
are swimming around him,
the wise before their time,
the voiceless, the numb,
only their faces visible
on the swirling water
of the river that has become the town.

By this time, the other actors
are circling Macbeth warily,
treating him as a madman
who has forgotten himself
in his part. His hair is wild
above his forehead,
a headland on the Baltic
crowned in stars, the leaves
of a tree of bitter summer.
Macbeth rushes up to the players
as they step back and to the side,
and all that he never knew
is known to him:

his body is a black boat spinning on Whirlpool;
he is rowing from rocks into Ocean,
his mouth a salmon's, his hair
the wind through rags
on a post thrust in hard ground
before the gates of a city,
the damp that people live in
who are the name of the sea,

who have walked out a free people,
who have named the stars,
who have given birth to the world.

Oh What Fools These Mortals Be

Phoenix Summer Theatre, 1975

Today Robin Goodfellow is a cox's orange pippin,
nestled among leaves.

The sun glints off a sheen of wax.
The scent of bees wafts from heavy grass.

Robin is waiting, waiting, waiting.
He swells around the sweet juice

in the languages of men — in this moment
together we are the language of birds,

and you who I am are surrounded by students
on a wooden stage; they are dressed in gauze;

they speak their lines so seriously
it's as if they had become books.

All the time Robin hangs from the lights,
sometimes by the crook of a single toe,

and whispers and buzzes and crackles and laughs —
bright fire on a summer night.

Robin can take on all the parts:
the heartbroken men from the boarding house,

Hermia who puts it out every night in the dorm,
her skin like butter melting in the mouth.

Smoochie, smoochie, mouths Robin,
almost losing his balance.

Shhhhh! softer on that footfall.
You're supposed to sound like a faery,

a garland around a girl's throat,
green stem to white blossom.

Look! Here comes Theseus,
king of the ape men,

dressed in his tights and his cape,
with his voice dropped down low

like the bottom of the sea,
leading a bull by the nose

through the circles of the mind,
la de da. God, pretty Lysander,

look at him! He's hung like a horse. Jesus!
Instead of him, the audience sees some farm kid

dressed in tights
and makeup like splintered glass —

reds and yellows and greens across his face,
his hair a bird's nest in an apricot tree

in late October, when the storms come
and the heart shivers

and crawls down into the feet
and will not budge.

Good god, yells Robin,
swinging down from the light bar

and landing on the stage with a thump
as the kid sweeps the stage clear

and the lovers have found each other
and embrace. Actually, if you see it from the back,

Demetrius is groping Helena
and she is sliding into the crook of his arm,

her breasts warm, her thighs
like the first page of *War and Peace.*

Ah, it really is a world of such promise,
winks Robin, copping a feel, then turning.

Can that actually be me? A soft whisper.
Running his green fingers over the boy's soft cheeks.

And just for a second
Robin has a shotglass of pity

and speaks out of the boy's voice,
If we have offended,

then breaks into laughter,
and skips off,

leaving the boy on the stage,
confused and alone with a set piece.

"Give me your hands
and all is mended."

God what is that supposed to mean?
But the crowd with their la de da claps,

and the men from the rooming house
wave from the front row,

with their grey faces
and the treacle on their teeth.

The tree goes out. In the darkness a bird trills.
The orchard is all around,

empty; the mountains rise up,
as if you released a spring

in the back of a picture frame
made of pipe smoke,

in which black and white people
stare out quizzically. Years later,

the dark voice of Oberon calls out to the boy,
Theseus dressed in drag,

and sometimes in the night,
when the world is still

and all the voices that make up memory
are off to the thickets of the forest,

the boy hears a small voice cry out
from the gold leaf pressed into the frame,

Captain of our fairy band!
Helena is here at hand.

And the youth mistook by me,
pleading for a lover's fee.

The light over the trees
that stretch around the you I am

sparkles like waves on the water,
until Robin comes over

and closes your eyelids with his finger,
and the last you see is the darkness,

and the last you taste is an apple
warm in the sun.

The Tragedy of Polonius

Thrift.

In the theatre of trees,
I am staging Hamlet
with a boreal forest
to replace the crab-clawed sea.

Instead of the battlements of Elsinore,
I have employed a grove
of dead spruce and the slap
of a beaver on still water.

Just last night, the watchers
on the battlements
had rehearsed the opening scenes
with halls of mirrors,
gem-encrusted swords, a crown,
and the traditional sweetmeats
stolen from the prop table
backstage to tease the king.

Purple with rage, the king ran
back and forth in the prop room,
looking for pastries behind curtains,
in the box with the rapiers,
even underneath Yorick's skull.
Tonight the watchers fight through undergrowth.

Ten minutes in, not one scene has come off:
no ghost has appeared;
Hamlet hasn't shown up backstage at all;
when Polonius calls his daughter,
to counsel her against a world of appearances,
she is nowhere to be found:
there are no tower apartments.
Second growth rustles above the seats.
Birds flit between dark branches.

Tears stream down the old man's cheeks.
Playwright! he shouts. *Playwright!*
He gestures wildly, then drops to the soil.
Just last night the director sat here;
there were lights; scripts were passed
from hand to hand; blocking diagrams
were annotated one last time.

Now there is the wind through the needles:
nothing nothing nothing nothing nothing,
no king, no queen, only one wrinkled old man
who came to be onstage, but has found instead
there is no stage in the world
and on the stage no world at all.

The Tragedy of Ophelia

Hamlet Redux

In Denmark, Ophelia hears drumbeats
deep in her sleep;

she wakes to the sea
crawling over crumbling capes,

a thousand soldiers dressed in black,
each with a skull on a stick,

swaying before the castle walls,
staring up at her without breath.

All the time, the roar of soldiers
drinking with the king snakes

through the corridors,
until it is the voice of stone.

The moon lies broken on waves.
It breaks on shore in foam and a hiss.

Ophelia has no power in this place,
but what power is here

paces through her sleep:
the prince on the parapet,

a ghost army in the fog,
led by a shape she cannot see.

She dreams it is herself.
She dreams the castle would vanish,

but when she opens her eyes
again to duty,

the prince is pounding on her door,
telling her to wake, telling her to sleep,

she does not know what he is telling her,
only that there is a river

flowing past her window, brown and strong,
and a city stretching over low hills.

She is thrown onto a stage
in front of a crowd yelling English,

like a bear in a pit,
a captured Pictish princess painted blue.

The crowd roars. This is her tragedy,
and even it has been stolen from her.

The only words she can speak
do not touch her words at all.

She is hustled on, she is hustled off.
Some idiot dressed as the king

brushes her ass with his thigh
and licks her ear. The drums beat in her sleep.

A ghost walks, carrying a chain.
He dumps it on her bed. It is made of words.

Hamlet's
father

A voice hisses in her ear,
lie still as if you are dead!

She looks up with a start.
Sitting on her bed is the prince.

In his arm is her severed head;
water pours out of his jerkin.

The room is flooded with the soldiers of the sea.
They jostle against each other,

trees in deepest winter,
without a hint of green.

And she was a maid once,
and ran out over hills among flowers.

What a sad prison is the prison of words,
where nowhere you turn is there action,

but everywhere there are the consequences
of action that remains unseen,

except by its shadows
and the words of ghosts.

Gertrude's Version

Hamlet (Hamlet's mother)

Gertrude is in the dairy room,
arranging flowers
and fruit
around her husband's body,
with cold water
running down the walls
and the smell of dark.

Beside her stands
a servant girl
from the village,
the blacksmith's daughter,
in her first blush,
her hair like rain —
hired by the king
with a nod
from his coach.

The girl is trembling
as Gertrude sticks
a newton pippin
in her husband's mouth
and slips a sprig
of parsley
into the grey hairs
around his prick. The apple
is warmer than the man,
she notes, and pauses.

There is the sound of breaking
chairs
coming from the main hall
and glasses
smashed into a grate.

The girl holds a candle.
She is only a face
rising above the light,
bleeding into darkness
at the edges
and reforming.

Gertrude remembers little
of her life
before she stepped
into this room —
how Raleigh came one afternoon
to the theatre
dressed as the sun,
and the Queen with him,
dressed as a spider
that had taken on the mask
of the queen of the fairies,
who takes lovers
as she will.

For a moment you could not tell
who was on stage and who
was the audience. When Gertrude saw
gold cloth sewn through Raleigh's jerkin,
she forgot her lines blankly.
Who knows what she said
in those few minutes
when she passed
from the South Bank of London
into Denmark and damnation.

The crowd roared.
She thought she heard fighting.
She was sure the Queen
came on stage
and switched places with her,
that Raleigh became king.

She no longer believes
anything can be set right.
She remembers city streets,
traffic, the long
yellow lawns of Hyde Park
rising into smoky air,
her childhood in the Blitz,
the empty blocks, smashed crockery,
crowds in Piccadilly Circus,
and the long years of absence and rain
when the greasepaint kept her sane.

That is all gone.
She is hiding in the cellar
with the corpse of a king
who stands on the top battlement
and crows at the rising of the sun
in a stain of blood
out of the sea.

The theatre has become a skull,
a toothless mouth, blind eyes staring
where there was a mind,
wind above a high path
over breaking waves,
and no expectation.
She hears laughter, the slippery sounds
of a man and woman fucking,
and the woman cries out —
she screams as she comes;
a shudder runs through cloven air.

In the silence that follows,
the world vanishes.
There is no servant girl,
no dead husband,
no castle. There is no candle.
The stars whirl around Gertrude.
A hunting bird screams at great height.
When the king steps up behind her,
as big as the sky,
to slip his tongue into her ear,
slipping his hands over her breasts,

she looks straight ahead,
where the sea breaks
against the castle walls,
afraid to turn.
If she looks into his eyes,
it will all become real:
she will forget even London,
she will forget she was a girl
who took to theatre
for poetry and the beauty,
the strength that came
from being the voice
of a poem itself
and the world.

And so the play will not pass its time.
The girl she was speaks, out of her fear,
of herbs and flowers
and healing, into the dark
where the audience once sat,

and hears out there a wild voice
slip down from tier to tier,
leap into the pit
and step across it slowly,
listening

greedily
for what she will do
now

that she is on her own.

- pivot point of book
- moment of free will
- free - anything is possible

TOM'S A COLD

—

I hope all will be well. We must
be patient, but I cannot choose but weep
to think they should lay him i' th' cold
ground. My brother shall know of it; and
so I thank you for your good counsel.
Come, my coach! Good night, ladies, good
night. Sweet ladies, good night,
good night.
– Ophelia

Desdemona's Wedding

Desdemona dressed in her grave clothes
for her wedding to the Moor, died her hair
pink and wore a pin in her tit, slipped
out of bed at night, wore studded collars
and crawled on her knees through stone streets
that night she married Othello .
and the sea fell to the stars.
Venice drew a cape around itself
and men drank it like wine
as the tide suckled their houses.

And even that happened too slowly.
Between jealous rage and a feather pillow
over lips that sought to speak a cry
of reason or a word of love,
whole centuries passed,
navies sailed out and sank in smoke,
armies bled in muddy streets,
men were dispatched like pigs,
Mozart composed his symphonies,
Beethoven went deaf, Schumann mad,

so don't say that thing
about Desdemona, that gossip about the Moor,
the right of conquest,
the soldier's lance, and don't ever
say the expected thing, that love is madness,
that the only madness is in the mind.
To have a mind is madness.
Pray you can hold out five minutes
between your wedding and your death.

The Mouse Trap:
Seventeen Stagings of a Play Within a Play

*The best actors in the world, either for tragedy,
comedy, history, pastoral, pastoral-comical,
historical-pastoral, tragical-historical, tragical-
comical-historical-pastoral, scene individable,
or poem unlimited.*

— Polonius

1. TRAGEDY

We sacrifice for the show,
sell tickets, dim the lights,
to watch young men — and women —
dressed in tights (or less),
or tarted up in golden skirts,
flirt with older men
and be riven down,
made to bow and eat their words, cry
out to gods praised nowhere
but in these tents beside the harbour
where young men fly kites,
brightly coloured, and women
walk their dogs,

not to be blinded and forget the shock
of first knowing that knowledge
is not more but less, but to bear
witness and condemn
the betrayal that bursts from every word
they speak and have not yet learned.
That's up to us. A tug

toots in the harbour, a siren whirrs past
on a nearby street, and the men in tights
sweat and practise death.
Bastards that we are, we clap.

2. COMEDY

Stars wink between high branches.
The moon rises over water,
containing love won and lost —
by the young. They betray themselves —
look how he rushes into her embrace,
but calls her false — or are betrayed
by those who've seen it all fall apart,
the young wife battered or the old wife left,
the pregnant daughters hounded by their shame,
and know all love will only last
if made from duty. (They're wrong
in that. We're right to be enraged.)

We who watch from the half dark,
strangers breathing the same breath,
know both sides — the fair young maid,
the coupling beast that rocks and cries —
yet cannot touch, cannot shout advice,
Turn around, she is your life!
We must watch in horror as the worst
we always feared becomes the best
and the best, if not the worst, at least
too much like us for us to sit
in comfort on our hard chairs and do less
than praise the way they find each other,
these tyrants of the heart — and are lost.

3. HISTORY

The wise plod. Oh, there was Herodotus,
boar hunting on Mount Ida. That kicked our story off —
and wars, navies ambushed in the straits,
the prince who rode a thousand leagues to subdue the East:
justice bought with slaughter. We can buy that, nod,
and whisper to each other across the aisle.

They call it honour. We have dressed
in our best thought, heard the speech
the dramaturge made outside the tent
before the show began, how the heart
is governed by the state,
the state is measured by the heart,
and natural justice is a wheel, that turns,
grinding flour from our supple bones.

I'd rather think this is a court,
and we who clap the jury and condemned at once,
who must decide which role we'll play
before the play is done, the wheel stops
where we are, and we stop this play
to plod out to the slaughter.

4. PASTORAL

The sun is an ancient voice,
slow footsteps tapped in music, the god we are,
that first spoke words on a stage
of stone so we who play hide
and seek with guests
beneath the trees will know
the ends that words will make
if given space. Time's
what we do not have — what passes for it
moves slowly as if catching us from behind;
out of breath, we let ourselves be caught,
and, man or god, that which catches us
is possessed.

Word sometimes comes of distant cities,
the rage of men desiring to subdue
and be subdued, and ships sometimes pass
on their way to war or struggling to find
some way back. To men who bear
such words and ride such ships
we who live here at a distance
can provide haven only if they forget
what no man can forget, the horror
he must witness when he takes a life,
and can provide few words — in fact have few —
and no answers. This is not a quest.

5. ROMANCE

We've all heard this story: the damask roses,
the tower window, the nightingale,
the dreamy view over lake and fields,
the prisoner in the dungeon tied to his chain,
all forms of contemplation of the name of God,
all forms of ecstasy, the girls
that wait upon a woman waiting
for a lover who is sheathed in iron
and at the wars where other women
who once waited, smelling roses
below their windows, sing their children
to sleep with songs of war,
Your father is in Pomerania;
Pomerania is burnt to the ground —
the ineffable distance that is God.

These are terms of endearment.
It starts out as a comedy,
the fools come on, do acrobatics,
and the crowd goes wild, cheering,
laughing, throwing hats
into the air. We are the crowd.

The playwright has not finished with us.
The play goes on, becomes a tragedy,
the woman damned by jealousy
to become a man, poison taken
that is not poison but the voice
of reason killing the self
so the self can live. To watch is cruel.

Better to stop laughing and pay attention
to the roses, their waft of cloves,
the sweet earth pouring up,
and focus on it, ignore the duke,
who passes laws, and pray —
you can hear the murmur of our discontent
like trees in an October wood, a hangman's moon —
that justice passed does not make fools of us,
that the twists of fate are more than twists,
but lead out of the maze to welcoming friends.

6. LYRIC

Children sing
tra-la-la-la
and sweet springtime,
dancing around
a pole with ribbons,
their faces scrubbed,
dandelions
glowing under chins.

They all love butter.
They know every word
to "Rain, rain, go away,"
but not yet hey nonny, nonny,
under the greenwood
tree with ravens.
There's time for that.

Oh, it will come.
They run now in the yard,
play prisoner against the fence,
and hurt the girls by holding
them against the wire
until "Georgie Porgie,
pudding and pie,"

but soon they'll run
out in the grass,
hair flying, arms bare,
the mountain sun
burning in their mouths
and lips and tongues
and all their fingers,
learning touch —
and they will sing,

oh they will sing
these words in all
they are and be
alive in this
as we are alive
in these words we sing
as the footsteps dance
and fall on grass
around the pole
that dancing makes
of our long life
and our short death
that dying makes.

7. EPIC

Our time is slow
and ponderous

as is befitting a journey deep
into the ritual telling

that makes a word speak
and speech mean.

We are, in all that
would destroy us and make us

destroyers of our selves,
lashed to a pole, taunted

by the god of the sea
on a dusty field

before a city, hearing words
no man can bear

to hear and not go mad,
giving death not ours to give — makers —

facing ourselves
over these words of polished bronze

that reflect a dream of us.
We return as strangers

to all we loved
and all who loved us.

Of this we speak,
using words that once were gods

to speak a human truth
the gods must hear. We are.

8. LIEDER

The silence
booms and shakes,
trapped in a mahogany
piano case
that is nailed shut
with little hammers
trimmed in felt.

There is a pounding on the lid,
from inside out.
A trout, you think,
my god, a trout!

It rills and trills,
a thin shrill voice
babbling of streams
and clear running water,
a brook,

to drag a word
from somewhere deep,
that is not water now
but the mind,
trying to get out.

We speak of nymphs,
locked into trees,
whose voices rustle
in the leaves,

of swallows,
dipping, crying
in high light,
who are also voices
become the earth.

That's the way it was
when we first knew love.
Now the earth becomes us.

We sit in rows,
dressed in black and white,
without a sound,
to watch the coffin boom,

a woman lean
beside it, singing it
into a voice
that makes a shape
that we can hear
because it's us,

and a man in black
with swallow tails,
pressing keys,
so seriously,
with a nudge and wink.

Being who we are
at this funeral for the solemn
frolic of the earth,
we accept that what

he plays is not water
and what she sings
is a fish,
and that there are words for this.

When they're done
with this circus act,
we stand and clap
and call for more,

and more and more.
Again the polished coffin shakes.
The people in there
are trying to wake.

9. MORITÄT

Every dead man deserves the chance
to sing on some rickety stage in a backstreet pub
and set us straight. It's best to ham it up —
no one stands in judgement now except the living,
and they aren't worth a damn once we're pushing
up the daisies. Death we remember. It's living we forget.

That's common sense and all sense is common
where we end up, so celebrate the lives you took
to make a buck, the cement boots you gave the men
who stole your turf for fifty grand and the others
who owed enough to kill for you and keep you clean.
Now you can sing it all. Tonight's the night. It's grand!

It's best to keep the noose around your neck —
a morbid touch, for sure, but striking — and to laugh
at the drunks who sit and stare and clap, clap, clap,
for they've learned like you, far too early,
that life's a bitch, fuck her, and you did

and now she's fucked you over good.
Ah, that's the life. Sing it now. Come on. Whip them up.
Where they're going they'll forget the drink,
the shit they took to get them here, but this,
so sweetly sung, they won't forget.
Goddamn, you owe them that much.

10. DIRGE

Our dreams cannot sing.
A wolf howls on a hill.

A horse stirs in a stall.
A man weeps in a bed.

A bed falls through the floor
into the darkness of the heart,

to use an old way of talk,
which I use now,

having been through gladness
at the start

and having seen it through.
This is the end.

Now we can really talk.
The door knocks on the door.

This too is old
and speaks that way.

It speaks to us,
not to itself.

A cat stares through the glass.
A woman walks through water

to the trees.
She doesn't come back.

11. KLEZMER MUSIC

Weeping is no use.
I am remembering how to dance a slow, dead
dance after a wedding
in the streets, candied roses, perfumed sheets,
as the blue sun rises over smoke
that rises from the river that burnt
all night and now is cold as ash and darkest dark.
Cold and blue, it flows out through fields
to the drinking sea.

I am going home with the other
drunks, our arms linked. The road's not straight.
We are dancing it. The music's in our heads,
that plywood violin, that stretched steel string,
the pipe, the bass, the voice that shrieks,
and wails and weeps. We are in love.

The bride was radiant, the singer tossed her breath
to us, tied up with ribbons and we caught
it while all the dead lined up in back
and clapped and tapped their wooden
shoes and played their ribs and plucked their teeth.

We've grown used to them, but they
have not grown used to us, the clumsy
way we walk back to our beds, the vodka
tossed that makes us sick,
and that other wedding where they will play for us.

12. TRA LA LA

What we hum is the shape we're in.
My grandma used to hum

romantic songs while baking bread.
If she sang or cried out loud

while making love, I can only guess.
I hope she did. The bread was good.

I hope she moaned and cried out love
once or twice to God because

she did not know more than scraps
of tunes. The words were lost to her — and us.

I am telling you these words you see
are only blanks for you to fill

with what you know to be the case
among the words that gather round

to peck the tra la la and la de da
she used to sing when feeding them.

She doesn't feed them any more,
so it's up to us. I miss her arms,

white with flour, the laugh that made
her shake and sit on wooden chairs

to catch her breath, and catch my breath
to think of it as you must think

what you will as you breathe
in and out while words cluck

and peck each other's backs
until they bleed and feathers fly.

13. ODE

Have you ever found yourself talking
to yourself and not knowing what
you were talking about at first,
then it slowly dawned on you
that you were going crazy because
when you were talking no one was listening
to a word you said and when you were
listening your words began to slow
and then to peter out; you looked
around to see if anyone in the room
had noticed — they had, staring at you, their mouths
half open, drinks raised, held just
inches from their lips, a knowing
look in their eyes you dared not answer
with the little you could still say? Me too.

They stare; I fall into all that has been
left unsaid between us and which we must
speak now in the little time we have left
or it will outlive us. It all happens so slowly:
my joy, my rage, fill me like water
poured into a cup and lifted to my lips,
like deer that have wandered in from the forest
to a glacial stream and look across
to the highway where trucks scream by,
tarps snapping at their ropes, and people
pass in cars, their lips moving without sound.

14. BALLAD

A horse stands in a field
beside the man it's thrown.
A woman kneels in prayer
behind her walls of stone.

Over the blackened moors
the stars set on the earth.
Under the burning roof,
the wind blows through the heart

that does not rhyme with man
when war is made and lost.
No man can find his home.
We who count the cost

travel down a road
made of bones and rust
and tally up the prayers
that prayer lift us up

over the blackened moors
until the story stops
because it's found an end.
The ending shocks.

When war is made and won
no woman finds the man
returned the one who left.
Since this story began

horses have run off
over a blackened moor,
the women who stayed behind
have grown hungry and poor.

We who tell this story
of true love lost
and found in loss
must pay the cost

of what we tell, while you
who hear must know
this story does not end.
It began and now

it is your story too;
horse and tower,
woman, man and field
are in your power,

not mine. Tell them.
They are the world you know
and lose through love
and they lay you low.

15. GRIEF

It is the way we make what is be what we are,
however briefly, however we may aspire

to more than sobs that shake us loose
of what we were and what we will become,

to hold us here just a little longer,
where we don't understand what brought us

to this stasis and this end, how the tumor started,
spread, the black hours beside the bed,

the meters, tubes, the nurse who comes
with catheters, morphine, a low voice, rubber shoes,

day and night, calls us gently by the name she knows us
by, until she comes one night before the dawn,

pulls the plug, brushes down the lids,
while we sit among the flowers we have brought

and all the symbols of a life now passed
we cannot find our way to down any hall.

No door leads out. The doctors nod.
We don't wander out but in.

It is our grief we become at last,
and all who see us in the next weeks,

our eyes bloodshot, living on pills,
giving a speech to friends in a windy field

because she would enter no church
where the voice was caged, sprinkling ashes

to be caught and blown away into the unsayable,
signing papers, reading wills,

packing her clothing in a box
and lying in the empty bed that was a field

of roses and now is cold as snow,
do not see the lives we were,

the death we have become, but the door
that swings between them both and lets us in

to let us out. We are wandering now, out in the snow,
while the world sleeps, free of pain,

and dreams at last the dream of knowledge
we can only grieve.

16. WHY DO NOVELISTS HAVE ALL THE FUN?

They plot their lovers with thumbtacks
on their walls and type not to learn
but to fill in the blanks.
Here, there are just blanks,
which novelists fire from a gun,
bang bang you're dead, ho ho,
now you jump up. It's temporary.

They write of detectives in shabby offices,
their names stencilled on frosted glass,
following the cheating husband,
the emerald thief, because that's
where they live and we always write
of what we know best.

In this house, for instance, no sooner
do we get one thought to follow
another so they begin to make some sense
of us and what we're doing here
(it's intimate) than the novelist
knocks on the front door, wearing an overcoat,
a felt hat, and making cracks
from the side of his mouth.

If they really want, they can watch.
It's not true that they have all the fun,
but we won't tell them who your husband is,
who my wife, what the silence does
for you, what it cost, or what ship in the harbour
brought it in. Let them imagine that
and have some fun.

17. WHAT IT IS

Not magicians with hats inside rabbits,
nor *Can you pick the ace of spades?*
I'll saw you in half now,

though it could be that, it could be
anything we wish to burn our fingers with,
lighting the candles on a cake

that was once the moon, sparklers on Halloween,
bean seeds cast on a red cloth
when a squirrel runs across your path

in Guatemala, the way the birds
that are speaking from poplar to water willow
are flying like a book, the way

that inside what says *we* there is something
which we said and is us more
than anything we could divine.

Who are we when words become
our names and the names of things
put on a black tux and laugh out loud

under the lights, with eggs
in their ears and gold coins
under their starched collars

and clinking inside your left pocket
with your keys, except poetry,
our shocked ends and beginnings?

Give Me Your Hands

In this moment Puck is a broom
he uses to sweep the floor of the stage.

For his last trick, he sweeps himself away
with one hand,

while holding the broom with the other.
There has been a wedding here today,

the clay floors laid with rushes.
Evil spirits cannot enter:

there is nothing old that does not vanish
as quick as a gesture.

Evil spirits are camped in the doorway,
laughing at the groom, grinning

knowingly out of faces of ash,
humping each other,

with an expression on their faces
of complete absence.

Soon there is nothing on stage
but the echo of Puck's presence

and the bang of the janitor
locking the front door.

In the swelling darkness, the things
laugh onto stage with brooms of their own

to set up the whole play again,
perfect right down to the braying of the ass,

but in the darkness, without light,
played solely by touch.

Oberon is the most magnificent,
a black beetle unfolded in light from a window;

he is tireless and possesses everyone,
from the fat boy who plays Mustardseed,

to the old man who mimes Theseus
and smells like a bull.

When the actors come again in the morning,
with their ragged clothes and their breath of milk,

the stage is empty — there is not a footprint in the dust.
They begin immediately to rehearse,

so they don't forget their lines at night,
which is always the greatest danger —

remembering that they are playing a part,
which the midnight actors are dying to forget.

Phoenix Theatre, Victoria, 1975
150 Mile House, 2003

ABOUT THE AUTHOR

Harold Rhenisch's poetic roots stretch across Canada, to Eliza-
bethan and modernist poetics, and into East European imagery
and symbolism. The grandson of German refugees, he left the
orchards of British Columbia's Similkameen Valley in 1975 to play
Puck in *A Midsummer Night's Dream*. Returning to the Similkameen
in 1982, he wrote of his land in five meditative books of poems, con-
cluding with *Dancing With My Daughter* and his innovative prose
autobiography, *Out of the Interior*. The theatricality celebrated in
Free Will first found shape in his 1998 collection *Taking the Breath
Away* and its companion collection of trickster poems, *The Blue
Mouth of Morning*. His prose works have related his oral culture to
global issues of language and renewal, including his novel *Carnival*,
which leads a boy out of a world of myth during World War II, and
his *Tom Thomson's Shack*, which portrays Canada from across the
rural/urban divide. The closing section of *Free Will* follows Rhenisch
back to the "British" in British Columbia, introduced in "On the
Couch of Dr. Daydream," his translation of ten Shakespearean
erotic sonnets into Canadian English. A companion poem from
this series won the Arc Poem of the Year Prize for 2003. Rhenisch
lives in 150 Mile House on British Columbia's Cariboo Plateau.